The Matrix Exposed°

Unplug from ties that bind you
Unlock keys to a Magical Existence

By Katrina Loukas

"*For those who are ready to hear it and are seeking spiritual growth, it is amazing! I've felt so bubbly and happy all morning and I swear it's because I am focusing all of my energy on ME. I can't explain it, but there's a spring in my step and I feel really light and free and I honestly feel it's form what I learned form your book .. about freeing myself from the matrix!*"

– Kate

"*Your Book Rocks! Even with all of my experiences, and of all the theories on resolving cords that I have tried, none have been as effective. I felt the coolness as the cords dissolved, and a relief with peace.*
I Love you, and thank you so much. I have already recommended your book to a dear friend in California, who needs the guidance, and others. I hope they order it now!"

- Holly

Published by:
Katrina Loukas of Sacred Mysteries

Visit http://SacredMysteries.com.au for more info.

👍 Like Us on Facebook: Sacred Mysteries Facebook Page

👍 Join our private Facebook tribe (by request only): The Power Pack

Join our private membership club, The Hood, for authentic co-creation: http://SacredMysteries.com.au.

"Katrina is science and magic. She is incurably wise, playful and fun. She brings me joy and rattles my cage in the most delicious way. I love the way she addles my mind with new paradigms."

Kim, Sutherland Shire, Australia

"Katrina, ... I did not think someone could get to the heart of things in such an approach, yet I found out that what you do is remarkable... I have NO hesitation in recommending you to people. What you do quite quickly uncovers that which has been hidden, that no longer serves a person...and in the uncovering you take people to the next stage of release just as effectively."

Mark, Sydney, Australia

"(Katrina) ... was brilliant! ... It's amazing how quickly she uncovered the truths of it all by watching my hand signals. "

Kylie, Cronulla, Australia

"It was lovely to meet such a beautiful soul that exudes a wanderlust and strength in areas that the most fearless won't go. You are very special."

Marie, Beecroft, Australia

"Katrina clearly has a love for mankind and more so for the well being of all mankind. Her pragmatic, no-nonsense, empathetic approach cultivates results and from areas that come as complete surprise. My initial question was to Katrina was: how do you tie the soul stuff we all work on

with the head stuff??? I now know!"
Tom, Liverpool, Australia

*"Destiny placed this gentle luminous soul in my path –
intuitively I knew there was a reason I was very drawn to
her wisdom and her incredibly warm heart. It's all about
the heart with Katrina :-)."*
Carla, Marrickville, Australia

*"Katrina was able to quickly and intuitively diagnose the
root cause of my situation, and offer both practical and
spiritual solutions. At all times I felt a genuine warmth
and compassion from Katrina, backed by a solid intellect
and perceptive presence. I would recommend Katrina to
anyone seeking fresh and effective ways forward from their
current challenges!"*
Peter, Robinson, Australia

"At a time when I experienced very sudden and surprising shock and grief, Katrina's care was truly authentic and invaluable to me. I am so grateful for her genuine concern for me. It has touched me very deeply. In addition to this, her wise mind and heart have helped me begin to unravel the meanings and lessons in the pain. She holds a bright light for what is possible, and when my own hope wavers, I know she holds the light for me, until I can find it within myself again."

Anonymous, Sydney, Australia

"By allowing me to get in touch with my soul's essence, Katrina has helped to expand my self-awareness and develop my own spiritual path to healing. I would not be where I am today without her guidance and she will continue to play a vital role in my journey to recovery and self-discovery. "

Kate, Sans Souci, Australia

Dedication

Every woman has an alchemical key.
That only her beloved can unleash.
My twin love,
This Sacred Knowledge is our golden child
Conceived through the mirror of your soul.
A Bridge to connect humanity to
The Magic of their Divine Birthright;
During those moments of bliss
When we became one with all Creation:
You Unleashed My Key.
A key that unlocked
Powerful Wisdom
Born to free humanity
For good.
God bless your soul contract.
With All My Timeless Love,
- Katrina.

"Each moment one has to be at ease with oneself - not trying to improve, not cultivating anything, not practicing anything. Walking is Zen, sitting is Zen, Talking or silent, moving, unmoving, the essence is at ease.
The essence is at ease: that is the keyword."

- Osho

Preface

On the 19th of April 2014, after an evening of profound connection with my beloved, it came to me in deep contemplation, that I had conceived. Indeed, in the weeks that followed, I felt impregnated and worried, "oh this can not be"!

Two weeks later Spirit said "his name is Bridge and OPTIMAL for the human race". I responded in full devotion to my mission: "I agree to this".

I'll never forget this moment. It was while I was driving home from work, and a second after hearing it, I drove past a black car with the word *'optimal'* painted in big green letters along its side. And even though I did not doubt it, I still got goose bumps let me tell you! From then on I was certain Bridge was to be.

Alas, it wasn't a physical child at all and so I parked this gnostic mystery – for embracing the liminal space of not-knowing is surely rewarded with the gift of knowing – when the time is perfectly so.

When one learns to simply tango between the two pillars that are Knowing and Not-Knowing, Grace surely arrives at their door.

Fourteen months later, during a self-healing session, I had a vision where the 'head physician' of my 'Spiritual Healing Team' handed me a **golden baby**. From this, I was certain - Grace did not let me down - I was going to finally give birth to 'Bridge', something special and divinely inspired. And so I lay in wait, bubbling with nervous excitement.

A week later, on the 22nd of June 2015, The Matrix Revelation, on which this book is based on, came to me. This marked the crowning of Bridge: who turned out to be a healthy bundle of 7 Sacred Keys and Wisdom Knowledge that lay deeply locked within my DNA code, whose seal had finally been broken. I was then guided: "And now you write".

And so it is that the words you are reading will weave their magic into the cauldron of this book. This book, and the others to follow form a golden key, an artifact, born to unlock the puzzle of your existence.

So I gift you the debut of Bridge, and wish with all my heart that you, a sacred instrument of Divine creation, may thrive and live life to your deepest desire – free, unbound and whole.

With all my love,

Katrina xox

- Katrina Loukas

Founder of Sacred Mysteries

Introduction

So you've probably been on this journey for some time now. Some people call it a spiritual search, some an awakening, while others call it self-improvement, personal growth or development.

Do the words really matter? They simply come from different mindsets, that's all. Because essentially, we all seek the same thing.. But what is it we seek?!

How did this journey begin for you? With the most subtle of inner nudges? Something from within, pushing you to shift 'stuff'?

Oh and the methods vary for each of us: meditation, yoga, inspired quotes, books, courses, motivational speakers, energy healing, psychologists, medication, astrology, numerology, psychics, coaches, the gym, the pub, Facebook, a church, a club, a group, a fad, an affair - whatever has tickled <u>your</u> fancy – as sparked on by that NUDGE.

And it's all been worth it to some extent, I know it has.

But still that nudge remains… Still that subtlest of un-ease lurks in the undercurrents of your every day and you have no clue how to permanently appease it. It's as though a relentless pet dog keeps bugging you to pat him but you want to just get on with things and move on with your life.

Of course, you've nailed it many times, shifted the 'stuff', conquered the nudge – only for it to then come back and haunt you once again. You've had the fleeting moments of clarity. Thing is: every therapist, medical practitioner, beer, chocolate, gym session – has only ever provided TEMPORARY RELIEF, just as panadol only provides temporary relief for headaches; so too have any of these only provided temporary relief from this subtle yet unrelenting NUDGER.

So you remain, perplexed…

My beloved reader, I sincerely hope that the revelations in my writing will provide you with the insights you need to free your self of this incessant nudge. But be warned: the journey is not for the faint-hearted.

Now I ask you to walk with me, along this final leg of your pilgrimage as a 'seeker', where you will get to not only understand, but LIVE exactly what IT is that your essence has been seeking for so long.

Housekeeping

Sacred Keys

 Throughout this book you will find this image. It signals that the information next to it is highly valuable. I call these whopper nuggets of wisdom 'SACRED KEYS'.

Jargon Smasher

Shining the light of unity consciousness across the diversities of human existence, quite often sees me **smashing down the barriers caused by JARGON**.

The paradox is that, when you do that, you begin to form your own jargon, the beauty of this being that you can then smash it down again at your leisure! Just as children at play build something with such passion, then smash it down again in an instant. This is not crazy – this is being EMERGENT, remaining EVER-PRESENTLY YOU.

So without apology, here are some words, phrases & concepts I use synonymously that **without the barriers of a mindset, mean the same thing**...

Table 1: **Words Without Borders**

Words & Concepts	Essentially the same thing:
Self-Improvement	Spiritual Journey Personal Growth Self Mastery - but here the goal is attaining the ultimate 'Level of Consciousness' possible for a human
Energy	Power
Your Vibe	Your Energy Body
Spiritual	Quantum
Individualized Consciousness	Your Higher Self Your Quantum Self
Essence level of existence	Energy level of existence

Self Mastery - Living In Your Zone of Genius

The purpose of this book, and others to follow, is to help you reach the utmost level of consciousness while still inhabiting a human body. I call the path to this, 'Self-Mastery'. It is the ultimate destination for those committed to self-improvement; when YOU are the master of your existence such that your life is in abundant flow in love, money, work and joy.

This **magical** way of existing *is* possible, as Gay Hendricks, in his best-selling book 'The Big Leap' confirms, calling it "Living in your zone of genius".

To reach this level, you must consciously work on how you relate with your: physical, emotional, mental, and energy bodies (amongst other things).

You must also aim to **align** your four bodies (loosely speaking there are 4), so that they work together as one – coherent and harmonious. When they work wholly in alignment their connection to your Individualized Consciousness is at optimum capacity.

At the moment, we are like mobile phones whose connection bars are always on low. We have no chance of getting clearer reception to our Individualized Consciousness with our four bodies out of sync like this.

The important thing is, to align your bodies, you need to work from the outside inward, from the Energy Body in towards the physical body. This is because any dis-ease at that level filters down into the physical.

In actual fact, our Energy Bodies need rehabilitating. We need to re-train our Energy Body not to: leak energy to others unwittingly, nor carry it for others unnecessarily either, to increase it's ability to generate energy naturally, and to lift its vibe to optimum capacity.

I call this '**Energy Mastery Training**', and the actual exercises on the Energy Body I call '**Energy Work**'. Indeed, there are ways to train the Energy

Body, just as there are ways to train your physical body.

In other words, you must remember this:

IT ALL STARTS WITH ENERGY!

The Matrix

You have been trapped in a Matrix.
For thousands of years this Matrix has bound many
of you to the earth realm in endless karmic cycles of
torment and suffering.
Across the wilderness of the Universe I heard the
yearnings of your souls.
Like a drum beat strumming it's despair;
Leaving my mystical heart beating in-tune with your
longing.
And so it was that I came to be:
To bring forth the Sacred Knowledge,
So that you may emerge, boundless,
To play limitless and free amongst the stars and the
heavens;
To revel in the delights of abundance once more.
A reality your hearts have always known...

Katrina

Start with the End in Mind

On the eve of writing this book, the sacred mystery that is the Universe gifted me a rich confirmation for it.

During that day, as I was pottering around my home, I began wondering silently in my head: where *did* that spider go? I'd seen it a week earlier, but it seemed to have disappeared since then. All I could recall about it was that it was *huge!*

That evening, as I went to pick up my journal I felt something squishy underneath my thumb, on the front cover. When I looked down, the mystery of the spider was solved – it was dead, under my thumb!

Me, a petite 5'3", had squished it dead without even realizing it! Can you believe it? Out of all the possible spots it could have been in my house that evening, it just happened to be right where my thumb was going to be when I picked up my journal! That poor spider!

What intrigued me though, was that I was not at all freaked out by this – as I previously would have been.

I had been contemplating our collective's irrational fear of spiders for a while, and my gnostic wisdom told me it alluded to a fear of our own deep inner spiritual power.

I could see how this could be so. After all, once you connect to your true spiritual power, you realize how scary it would have been to connect to it any sooner than what you had... We only meet what we're ready for after all...

It was then that I realized this event marked something BIG. Killing the spider meant that not only had I conquered the scary task of owning my spiritual power, but I was going to help others do so too, through my writing amongst other things.

The mystery did not stop there of course! Because, get this – I was calling The Matrix a WEB in my 'brain dumps' - for this book!

The important thing is, I was feeling so out-of-sorts since The Matrix revelation several days previous, that I had lost the certainty of how to merely dwell within my body; for, I was not sure who I was, what I wanted, where I wanted to go, who I wanted to be.

Indeed, I'd been in a similar place before throughout my process of awakening, but this was of a much more profound, more permanent nature. And, although I felt liberated, unbound, and free beyond measure, I was simply traversing unchartered territory. I was on my own, with not a soul I knew in my predicament.

My previous existential framework, about needing to know - what I wanted, where I was going, and how I was going to do it – simply would not hold for long at all. It was quite perplexing, and very perturbing –

my mind was just at a blank! Because, I was, simply EMERGENTLY ME, in every moment, emergently me.

I could not force myself to answer any of those questions my process of existence on this planet had previously thought was mandatory to do so. Because I simply **did not know**.

All I did know was my experience - that my internal world waltzed in harmony with my external world. They simply danced together, meeting each other equally, exchanging information, reshaping my experience, and then again and again and again...

There was more – I felt the strongest of energy pushing up from my torso, through my throat, up into my third eye, then shooting out through my crown, more than ever before. I asked, "what is this?" The transmission received was, "We need to get the data from you, lots of it, from this, a rare human experience, for so long".

It was then I realized how deeply we all have a purpose. And it is not simply one way – we come here to also gather data, to send back up, in order for the expansion and growth of the universe, as well as ourselves.

From this moment on, my doors have truly opened up to the Universe. I have experienced being a Universal Citizen beyond anything I've ever known. I am connecting, on a deeper and deeper level, with my non-earthly counterparts who work for the highest good of all. I am also in connection with my other 'selves' doing their 'work' in different places across the Universe. Let me tell you - we truly are not alone. For those that think we are – um, well, that's funny and cute, but so 20th century!

The symbolism in killing the spider validated for me that, I, like my ingenious cousin the spider, am now intricately, creatively, spectacularly, **organically engineering my own web, my own matrix**; and that in THIS sheer fact – I truly am – the MASTER OF MY OWN UNIVERSE.

This was validation indeed: I had done it. **I had managed to remove any final ties I had to The Matrix, and that I was out!**

I could now set about weaving my own web through life, as I liked. That I, as my own master am in control of my own energy stock, my own energy field, my own existence.

Oh, and I must tell you – I also felt compelled to Google the symbolism of spiders. From this research, I found further confirmation – they represent creativity, especially for "those who weave their magic with the written word" (http://www.spirit-animals.com/spider/)!

I love when the Universe encourages us multi-dimensionally like this. Encouragement is such a valuable gift to a human, for I was encouraged to believe in my experiences and epiphany: that I had indeed unlocked **7 SACRED KEYS TO ASCENSION** for humanity. Keys that will JOLT people, propel them into true personal freedom, the likes of which they had forgotten was ever possible.

So now, I hope my words free you. I hope you too become a master in your own matrix, so that you can weave your own magical existence web, gifting us all the opportunity to behold the full glory that is you.

The Matrix Malaise

*"What you know you can't explain, but you feel it.
You've felt it your entire life, that there's something
wrong with the world. You don't know what it is, but
it's there, like a splinter in your mind, driving you
mad."*

The Matrix

SACRED KEY 1

 THE MATRIX EXPOSED: You have
been trapped in a debilitating
energetic Matrix for thousands of
years. This Matrix is the result of eons of
faulty energy exchange between humans.

It is a heavily polluted energetic field
engulfing the planet and you energetically.

Do you sense an 'urgency'?

This energetic pollution is increasing at an alarming
rate now, **because of the current system of
wireless technology on your planet. This**

network seriously compounds the affects of
The Matrix on you.

Matrix Definition

I am calling a matrix **an Energy Field that
surrounds a 'body'**. We each have a matrix as
does planet Earth. A healthy matrix should have no
'crossed wires' i.e. no 'entanglements'.

What I'm shown is that the eons of faulty energy
exchange has caused what looks like chaotic cross
wires going all over the place. This bungled mess is
causing huge disarray – not only for our planet and
her inhabitants, but also now universally.

It has begun to create a 'pull' to planet Earth, across
the universe, such that it is inhibiting the Universe
from its organic expansion process. Expansion is
actually what the Universe's perennial quest is all
about, as it is for us!

For our Energy Bodies, this current Matrix, feels like
a huge cloud of energetic pollution. It's pull is so

strong that it has been **sucking us into its bowels deeper and deeper like a ruthless vacuum**.

It is the reason you feel TRAPPED in something, but cannot pinpoint exactly what that something is. It is perhaps the main reason you've been nudged to find that 'release', that 'escape' - all along.

The Matrix has fogged your mental and emotional capacities as well as drained your energy levels. Even more so, it has obstructed the connection to: your self; others; the planet; the universe; and most importantly – **your individual consciousness**.

SACRED KEY 2

CORDS & CLUSTERS IN THE MATRIX: These eons of faulty energy exchange have created what looks like **energetic cables or cords linked directly from your solar plexus power source to two things: other individuals, and to congested clusters of mass consciousness.**

By mass consciousness I am referring to instances where masses of people have subscribed to belief systems that literally take their power, which is why we refer to them as disempowering! What these subscriptions have done is create energetic dense clouds or 'clusters' in The Matrix, that actually weigh it down even more – compounded by our hugely increasing population levels.

Many of our belief systems that we have subscribed to during our process of socialization, have inhibited our true individual potential. Examples of these include beliefs that hinder YOU around: education, law, medicine, relationships, money, the meaning of work, the concept of time, and so on.

These beliefs may still suit others, I am talking about the ones that may not suit you – or no longer suit you now, even if they once did. Because thing is, you may say you no longer believe in them, but if the energetic cords are still there, they are still taking your power supply, just without your everyday awareness realizing it!

The Cords and Clusters of Disarray

What I'm shown is that we have what looks like electrical cords attached to our energy bodies, stemming from our solar plexus (which is our power source), **connecting each of us to individuals AND to the clusters of mass consciousness**

The individuals are anyone **significant** in your life whether in your present or your past, such as: a partner, family, friends, teachers, Drs etc. Anyone in your thoughts, interactions – but especially those that have caused you 'grief', or that you feel 'bound' to.

These ties are plugged permanently into your energetic bodies, ready to TRANSMIT or RECEIVE power, or even CARRY the energy

of something that is 'unresolved' for those others.

The closer the 'tie', the stronger the cord -whether to a person or mass belief system

All these ties over all these years have together created this cloudy, heavy Matrix; the likes of which has sucked in the masses; into its entangled web of foggy disempowerment. Literally dis-em-power-ment – because your power (ie your energy) is PLUGGED INTO THIS FAULTY MATRIX.

It has trapped you, ensnared you, and kept your essence CAPTIVE in a perpetual sea of connection - FAULTY CONNECTION – for eons. It has kept you in mental disarray, interfered with your spirit connection, and caused emotional discord.

As such, it has disempowered you at a level you had never realized – the level of existence we are far removed from – the essence level. The essence level is the <u>energy</u> level of existence.

Stay with me, I will explain it all in detail as we go on.

What this has culminated in over all these years, is a heavily polluted suffocating energetic framework, the likes of which is now a huge web – a WORLD WIDE WEB - of faulty energetic TIES – connecting each of us here, there and everywhere. It is messy and it is overloaded. And your essence knows this, which is why you feel 'encaged', and want out!

This is why so many of us seek instant gratification, momentary release – our nudger's incessant quest: for ease.

Listen to our language: 'he fuels me', 'she drains me', 'she seems to take so much from me', 'I can't get over him, 'I feel bound to her', 'I feel like I owe him',

'I can't break the cord to her', 'he has a piece of my soul', 'I'm tied to it' and so it goes, on and on and on.

And it is because of this power leakage and energetic martyrdom, that so many attempts to feel better are NOT PERMANENT. SO many of our experts offer temporary relief – whether through medication or a prescribed set of tips and tricks – because they do not realize that permanent relief is possible, since they themselves are caught in this Matrix.

The good news is that there is a way out. And it all starts with energy. Before I go on however, I must stipulate a very important point: **since you are reading this, chances are you have already started – un-consciously – detangling yourself from The Matrix**. But, now that you know this, now that I'm 'bringing it to light' – what will happen is, that **the process will accelerate**.

Simply because your <u>conscious</u> self has become aware of it – so it's focus will send energy working away –

to unfold your release for you, **organically**. I hope you can start to see just what a true Creator you really are!

Why did this happen?

This faulty energy exchange happened simply because we humans forgot that ENERGY IS FREELY AVAILABLE ACROSS THE UNIVERSE; ABUNDANTLY SO.

SACRED KEY 3

 THE WAY TO EMERGE FROM THE MATRIX: There is a way to get you out of The Matrix; and that is for you to begin using the freely available Universal Energy as your only Power Source.

To tap into it – to work it, to use it, to harness it to build your own energy up - so then you have no more need for the cords and the respective power games that come with them.

This gets you out of The Matrix.

Now, I have formulated a simple way to do this, and I can share it with you – and it is the one I use with my clients.

But even more than that – I want this book to encourage you to trust YOUR WAY. To trust that your way of propelling yourself out of the stronghold of The Matrix by simply tapping into this free Universal Energy supply - is perfect and right – for you.

Now, it might include my Energy Mastery Training or being part of my Teaching Circles, or just reading some of the wisdom found in my books and posts.

But **I am not your end point**. I am only your Powerpoint.

For now.

Until you emerge yourself from The Matrix, you can revisit my words – and plug back in – to charge yourself up.

But rest assured, you will dissolve your own cage, and once you do, you will rise like a Phoenix out of the ashes of your experience; and then:

Emerge from the Matrix.

What is Free Energy?

Have you ever wondered where birds get their fuel to fly? Unlike an airplane, they don't have to get fuel injected into them to fly up in the sky...

Yes they are made to fly, but so is an airplane and I don't see it getting of the ground by itself.

No, what they use is the abundantly available FREE UNIVERSAL ENERGY, harnessed using a 'torus shaped' energetic 'vehicle'. The same energy that space ships must use to get to travel this far along the galaxy!

Now, do not be fooled, it is possible to create technology to harness it for us to use instead of petrol and electricity and what have you, however – this energy is not 'containable' – meaning: NOBODY can OWN it – so why would funding, research and utility overall – go towards something that is FREE?

And there you have the conundrum as to why our advancement as a race has bottlenecked – because there is no profit in it.

If you are interested to find out more about this and how there have been inventions ON THIS PLANET to harness it over the years, then watch the freely available 'Thrive the Movie' on YouTube. It is definitely mind-opening and I think you will love it.

Faulty Ties and Your BS Meter

"The Matrix is a system, Neo. That system is our enemy. But when you're inside, you look around, what do you see? Businessmen, teachers, lawyers, carpenters. The very minds of the people we are trying to save. But until we do, these people are still a part of that system and that makes them our enemy. You have to understand, most of these people are not ready to be unplugged. And many of them are so inured, so hopelessly dependent on the system, that they will fight to protect it." The Matrix

The reason The Matrix is faulty is because it is old-fashioned. **It is an outdated way of relating because it uses cords to connect us when the connection could be WIRELESS.**

It goes like this: remember how it was before rechargeable phones (some of you may not but bear with me!)? Our phones were not mobile, in fact, they were attached permanently to the wall – a CORD connecting them to the phone line system. So to talk on the phone we were stuck in one place, bound by that cord...

Then mobile phones came along, and we could connect wirelessly. In fact, wireless technology per se liberated us – it allowed us to work from home, well – it allowed us to work form anywhere in the world, study anywhere in the world, send documents to each other, send messages, have information at our fingertips, increase our buying power as consumers, create grass-roots movements that grow virally – the list is endless.

So, **the way we have been relating ENERGETICALY, is akin to pre-mobile days. We have been opening our 'fields' up so that we've had direct energetic cords linking us to each other**. This has been so for thousands of years.

These cords pierce our energy fields such that we leak our energy stock, and/or, carry energy for others.

I will be teaching more about how to combat this in my YouTube Channel and Blog so please stay connected with me!

All I want to say for now is this: this is a highly faulty way of relating for beings of consciousness as potential-bearing as us humans.

Furthermore, because this faulty energy exchange has been going on like this for so long, it has created this STICKY WEB, this heavily polluted FAULTY MATRIX system of energy that has: clouded our minds; entrapped us; and overly burdened our energy fields – leaving us with the most subtlest of inner unrest and unease; with great fatigue and exhaustion, with a need to escape, and, lost in a film of fogginess - for eons.

Basically, it has clouded our ingenuity, clouded our mental clarity, clouded our potential and actually 'dumbed us down'. And, we have finally had enough!

This Matrix IS THAT sticky web that has many of us seeking momentary relief in a myriad of ways, but for essentially the same reason!

I want you to know that: whatever you tried to do to relieve yourself from this unseen entrapment - whether meditation, alcohol, addictions, sex – whatever it was, it was because of this unrelenting self-propelling bid to escape the Matrix.

And it is time to get out.

You know this! This is why you are here, reading this book. Because you are ready. Ready to dis-entangle from this sticky web, to free yourself from this veil.

Ready for clarity. Ready for perpetual joy. Ready for true freedom; to embody real emPowerment.

Ready to simply EMERGE: **as YOU**.

Your BS Meter

What was the one thing that really got you here, reading this book? That really got you on your journey – that got the NUDGER nudging, got your essence at un-ease, got you looking at the big picture perspective, or questioning mainstream media, or any other 'authority'?

Your BS meter.

Your BS meter is that internal part inside of you that says "nope, I disagree"; that says "because I can"; that says "come on that's BS!"

It is your gut instinct, and it just KNOWS.

When it gets <u>stirred</u> it will <u>signal</u> to you via uncomfortable energy in motion (=EMOTION).

For example if someone makes an observation about you that sends your BS Meter into a spin with emotions such as bubbling annoyance, resolve or even anger – pay attention to it.

Practice, practice, practice! Practice listening to your BS meter and the emotions it stirs up in you; act on what it says – for example - by giving it a voice, as often as you can.

Even if you doubt it, still go ahead. Show it that you trust it. And, even if it's wrong once in a while, it does not matter – because, like anything you practice, you will get really good at staying connected to, and following, it.

Why should you do this? Because it is your advocate, your self-preserver. It has got your back, that's why.

Oh, and those people that de-authorize it – well, they are just the universe's way of providing you, along your unique path to self-mastery – an opportunity to PRACTICE listening to it. That's all it is.... So good luck – you can do it!

Where In Our Fields Are These Energetic Ties?

It is important to note that **these ties attach to anywhere in your field – probably where you might have a pain or two - but the real strong ones are often attached to our** HEARTS.

Know Your Power Source

The 'power' for your energetic ties comes from your central power source, which is located at your **solar plexus**.

For those of you that do not know where this is, it is in the stomach area, just under your diaphragm.

Which explains **the root cause of the GUT problems rampant today!**

Taking this one step further, it truly is suffice to say that The Matrix is the ROOT cause of our inherent un-ease; our **DISEASE.** Which means that if we want to really heal, we need to do so at the Energy Body level too...

SACRED KEY 4

IN DEATH DO US PART, SORT OF: The faulty **Matrix, over all these thousands of years, has gotten so heavy, become such a ruthless vacuum, that it actually pulls at one's energetic field even when they have passed on, making those energetic ties they have to anyone, or, to any system on the planet, difficult to break.** You can imagine then, why people have '**karmic ties**' with others from passed lives! Because they have an energetic cord literally linking them!

Or why people can be so entrenched in mass belief systems – again because they have these energetic ties to them, already linked to their energy fields before they come back onto the planet!

For those that feel that they have had many lives, that feel karmic ties still bind them, this Matrix is what has kept you stuck **within the confines of the earth realm** - reincarnating over and over again – trapped in karmic cycles - repeating the same lessons across many lives: because you actually have un-dissolved faulty energetic ties thereby keeping you in The Matrix even posthumously.

This brings me to **PSYCHICS and MEDIUMS**. Many people visit psychics and mediums to learn about loved ones that have passed, to learn about what will be in their own future even.

Let me tell you this: many of these psychics themselves have these energetic ties, not only to loved ones – but more importantly to mass belief systems that inhibit human potential. For example, most psychic's can only tap into the 'earth realm' – which is the realm closest to the earth - in which many departed loved ones reside (particularly those with ties to The Matrix). These psychics believe then, that this is where departed ones go, not realizing there's other more 'distant' realms further along, but that they simply cannot connect to the frequency of them. Thus their mindset is extremely limiting because thing is, if we have a powerful enough Energy Body, we can use it to soar to limitless heights when we 'die' – much further than the earth realm – since we literally have the POWER to do so.

[I will explain how to prepare the Energy Body for this posthumous adventure again through my channels so please stay tuned – I usually release the knowledge as I'm guided to do so to be honest – because you are ready to receive it and I am ready to give it! Of course, divine timing will dictate when this is to be so...]

So if you had a loved one that has passed on, please intend on freeing both of you from any energetic cords, so that you can both grow and expand, rather than keeping them tied to your grief, tied to the earth realm, they deserve to soar after passing on, beyond measure, in joy!

As for being able to see the future: quantum physics tells us that **everything exists as waves of possibility**.

So when a psychic is giving you a window into the future – **they are seeing what will happen along your current trajectory, should you remain on the current wave of existence you are surfing**.

This does not mean it is SET – which would be what you would believe if you had a TIE to the MASS VICTIM CONSCIOUSNESS that abounds on the planet today, that subscribes to the inherent belief that things 'happen to you'. In reality, things only happen 'to you' if you have something unawares about your Self, that is seeking to come into your everyday awareness. If you are Self-realized, you

Know that things do not happen TO YOU, but FOR YOU.

So what I am saying is, **you, as a master, can CHOOSE to surf a different wave** if the current one you are on is not serving your deepest desire, or – for those that want a full-volume magical existence – not in your ZONE OF GENIUS!

How Was It That I Could Emerge from The Matrix?

I realized that the reason I could come to this revelation about The Matrix and successfully emerge from it is because I have not had many lives in the last thousand years – actually there are two that I have been shown.

This has meant that that feeling of un-ease during this current incarnation for me, was SO FOREIGN, so UNNATURAL, to my usual state of Being, that I could not stop until I'd figured out exactly what was bugging me. Relentlessly so.

I always tell my clients to join all your dots if you want to know what your purpose is and how you will bring it. Because: **everything you've learnt PLUS all your character traits – make up YOUR dots**.

And your character traits – especially the ones you tried to push away because you were told to stop being so 'xxxx' – well, I call them your **superpowers!** All you have to do is master using them to yours and everyone else's benefits, and you have some power tools to work with there, let me tell you.

One big one for me was what I was told was my 'stubbornness'. No matter what I did, I simply could not stop it. I was stubborn, 'thick-headed' in that I would never believe anything anyone told me, if my BS meter could not digest it, even if it was an adult!; or I never swayed from my own inner knowing, no matter what the outside world dictated.

So, once I began to own my stubbornness, I was able to then use this superpower for the highest good of all. After all, it led me to some whopper insights like the ones you're reading now. And now I LOVE MY STUBBORNESS and I hope you come to love your superpowers too!

Another character trait of mine was this recurring embarrassing theme where there were certain things on this planet my brain just could not GET. Like sports for example - no matter how many times people would explain the rules to me, my brain could NOT process the information at all (ok and finance/accounting but sssshhh don't tell anyone about that one; oh and dates and time – I struggle with those two as well, how about you?).

This is because I have always framed things from a completely out-of-field angle – and these things just could not align with my out-of-fieldness.

I'll give you another (embarrassing) out-of-fieldness example of mine: one day I had gone to see a naturopath. After our consultation he turned to look at his computer, whereby he asked "Did you get us off the internet darl?" I replied in all my wisdom "No Tony, I didn't touch your modem."

This was following by a tangibly awkward pause between us – which gave me the chance to realize how stupid I had just sounded, and that I had probably just made it to his repertoire of funny client stories he shares at BBQs...

OK, so I hope you can see how embarrassing my lens has been for me throughout my life. I remember another time in 4th class answering a question and everybody bursting out in laughter. I had no idea what was so funny – even to this day... hmmm

Anyway, so yes, I am a 'newbie' to this planet and The Matrix. I must tell you now, many of you reading this may very well be too...

Our common traits include being: empathic ie super sensitive; warm hearted; wearing rose-coloured lenses for most of your lives, wondering just WHY aren't people smiling back?!; and: you KNOW you are here for a big reason - to help in some way...

If you can relate to any of this, then you are someone that has come to help with facilitating people out of The Matrix... so please join my private Facebook group called **The Power Pack**. Because I've been told it is time to start gathering the troops – people are almost ready for our help enmasse (but I know you already know this)!

Cord Types

The energetic ties attached to your energy field indeed strengthen over time. Through these ties we either **LEAK OUR POWER** or **SYPHON AN OTHER'S**. There are two types as I mentioned earlier: **collective cords and one-to-one cords**.

Collective Cords

Collective cords are created by mass consciousness. They are the **mindsets, or beliefs systems we give our energy – i.e. power - to**.

They cause **CLUSTERS OF DISARRAY** in The Matrix.

They have been **instilled (installed!) in us through our: upbringing, schooling, marketing, newspapers, the news, radio and so on.**

Basically what each cluster does to The Matrix is intensify its vacuum-ness even more. This is because each creates a distorting mass of heaviness in the field – they weigh it down. I'm shown they each look like a 'mass' that has a **'magnetic'** effect, drawing people into them - like the Bermuda triangle! Some are bigger than others, as you can imagine.

Many of these mindsets have just been inherited from the birth family and do not align with the individual's true being. And if this is the case, then they are truly limiting and as such, suck the power out of you **without you even realizing**; and have been doing so since your birth.

Subscribing to these simply is like plugging your power into them through an energetic cord. Which is why it is harder to extract your self from a collective belief system, since the **mass** of subscribers simply gives it that stronger **pull**.

Some current camps of mass consciousness come from subscriptions to: the victim consciousness; money as power; belief in lack; **any form of committed trust** without researching and/or acknowledging if something is **not sitting well about it IN YOUR GUT** – this quite often happens with the: medical system; a religion – whether it is around God, Science or Spirituality itself; the media especially mainstream radio, TV and newspapers; education; medical therapies such as pharmaceuticals, or alternative therapies for example – ANYTHING YOUR INNER BS METER ALERTS YOU TO THAT YOU MAY PERHAPS IGNORE TO KEEP IN WITH YOUR

BELIEFS, AND THOSE OF YOUR FRIENDS AND
FAMILY..

These camps really are as if we have clicked
'subscribe' to them when we own them as ours.
Importantly, this either leaks our power to them or
fuels us! Fuels us? You ask...

Yes, because, now if this is the case, there has to be a
two-way street between the camps. What does this
mean? This means there are **polar camps of mass
consciousness**! And **as one camp leaks their
power – they do so to the polar opposite
other**!

For example: subscribers to the poverty
consciousness fuel subscribers to the rich
consciousness; subscribers to the 'females as lower
rank ' consciousness fuel subscribers to the 'males as
higher rank' consciousness; subscribers to the
subordinate consciousness fuel the subscribers to the
authority consciousness. Other examples are: victims
fuel victors; feelers fuel thinkers etc.

The thing to get out of this is, if you can absolve yourself from subscribing to any of these warring clouds, then you are not fueling anyone!

Which means the more of us out of The Matrix, the less people fueling the power 'syphoners', and so the less power they have, meaning – they will eventually have no one to syphon from so will have to find a new, better game to play to exist.

One without division.

So, **getting out of The Matrix would not just benefit ourselves, but that it would actually benefit humanity.**

It would dissolve boundaries.

As such, it would actually **bring peace to the planet.**

This is why this information is so valuable and a way to free humanity. Because it works at the root cause of our current disarray – without weaponry, warfare or hurting anyone!

One-to-one Cords

One-to-one cords are of course to significant others like <u>current or previous</u>: partners, family and friends, abusers, bullies, authority figures – anyone you may feel 'connected with' even if you haven't seen them for a long time.

They may have verbally, physically or emotionally gotten to you. Once or many times. There may be trauma around them, or grief that will not go away.

They may be your mother, father, lover, husband, wife, daughter or son. They may be your best friend, nemesis, basketball coach, or personal trainer. Of course they could also be due to misappropriated power rank exchanged between, for example: Drs –

patients, teachers – students, policemen – criminals, priests – parishioners, managers – employers, etc.

And maybe, the incident or incidents that sparked the tie to them, may not have seemed a big deal to others, but nevertheless it was to you. This is what counts – because if it was a big deal to you, it means your energy has leaked to it!

If you find yourself: thinking about them, getting emotional about them, feeling irrationally triggered your whole life because of an incident with them – if you feel that you have a repeat button in your memory that just keeps getting pressed even when they're not in front of you, even by something unrelated – then you are energetically tied.

Someone is leaking, someone is syphoning.

Simple.

The important thing to remember here is that:

THE MORE ATTENTION, THE STRONGER THE CORD

There are ways to dissolve the ties. The 'how' of dissolving the ties I will discuss briefly in the next chapter, however, I do have plenty of videos in my YouTube Energy Mastery Playlist on how to do this. And I also send downloadable info-pictures (infographs) on how to break ties too through my email funnel so please opt-in for my Game Changers too.

Regardless, as I mentioned earlier, often times, we only need to realize something for it to then disappear soon after. So if you realize there are energetic ties to people or mass beliefs that you no longer desire, and you intend for their dissolution, then, as consciousness, you have brought this knowledge out of your shadows, into the light – for it to then be dissolved - for it's reason for existence is no more – you have outgrown it.

Waltz with a Vampire and Mambo with a Martyr

*"Love one another, but make not a bond of love:
Let it rather be a moving sea between the shores of
your souls."*

The Prophet, Kahlil Gibran

The collective and one-to-one cords have us repeating on autopilot two dance routines. These dances **keep the cords alive, strengthen them** and even more so – **drag us more and more into The Matrix**. They are:

1. The Vampire Waltz
2. The Martyr Mambo

For ease, in this chapter, I will address the one-to-one cords. However, you can apply the same principal to the collective camps, where each opposing camp do the waltz and mambo together, collectively.

The Vampire Waltz

The Vampire Waltz sees you trapped in the sway of either leaking your energy to someone and then, theirs to you. So that you take turns in being the vampire, sucking each other's energy as needed, through your little permanent cable to each other.

Your interactions see you going backwards and forwards emotionally entangled between say, at the extreme - bliss and hatred; at the more subtle level – niceness and passive aggressiveness.

Let me give you an example. For years I have had a friend I unwittingly danced the Vampire Waltz with. On one hand she would say hurtful things and I would be fueled by my anger and frustration. On the other she would 'pour her heart out' telling me how difficult her life was, whereby I would find myself trying to make her happy, to help 'take her pain away', feeling sorry for her, wanting to please her; going home feeling drained, exhausted and needing a nap.

Dare I say we were stuck in this waltz for many years, going backwards and forwards, twirling away lost in our little performances.

Until I realized what was happening. We were stuck in this little energetic dance! The way I realized it was one day only recently, when I heard myself say "I get so mad at her, she just fuels me"! There it hit me – I was getting energy from her when I projected her as my BUTTON PUSHER, just like she was getting energy from me when she played the 'victim' and I became the people pleaser!

You see, the truth when you see it through The Matrix is that I was being the VAMPIRE just as often as she was. Yikes!

Solution for The Vampires

So if you are in a Vampire Waltz that you would like to get out of, then all you need to do is:

ENDING THE VAMPIRE WALTZ

1. VISUALISE WITH FELT-INTENT DISSOLVING THE CORD TO THAT PERSON THAT CONNECTS TO YOUR SOLAR PLEXUS

2. VISUALISE WITH FELT-INTENT 'SEALING' THE 'HOLE' IN YOUR FIELD THAT CORD CREATED

The Signature of the Energetic Vampire

I thought I'd put together a sample list of tools we all, as energetic vampires, inadvertently use to syphon energy from others; in other words, this is how we KEEP THE CORD ALIVE **without realizing** we are doing it:

- Being apathetic by not showing interest or genuine concern
- Non-responses – to texts, emails
- Double signals: being hot and cold; warm and friendly then mean and nasty
- Using words as weapons*
- Inflating someone* over and above others
- 'Put downs', ridicule
- Mental 'power play'
- Judgements*
- Broken promises
- Knowing 'it all' and so interrogating others*
- Seeking sympathy*
- Playing the victim card:
    o Singing your own sacrifice *
    o Singing your own martyrdom *
- Performance* - eg dramatic expression
- Captivation* - eg dramatic expression
- Needing to please
- Being the one that 'tries to do the right thing'
- Overt incessant control*

* These tools are also used against the masses to keep their power plugged in to the clusters of consciousness through: the

media, marketing, news stories, religion; and systems such as education, medicine, justice etc…

Now, I do hope you can see that we've ALL been a 'vampire' somewhere along the line…

The Signature of the Victim

Here are some signs that your energy is leaking to another:

- Feeling drained
- Feeling bound to someone or to the event*
- Feeling that you 'owe' someone something
- Hearing yourself say things like: "he takes it out of me"
- Other possible signs may include: depression*, feeling down*, tears*, sadness*, mental replay over and over again, and obsessing.
- Any scenario where you leave feeling*:
  - Unheard
  - Undervalued
  - Invalidated
  - Disregarded
  - Disrespected

o **Unjustly treated**

* Signs that show you may be leaking your power to mass subscriptions too… Again your power gets plugged in through: the media, marketing, news stories, religion; and systems such as education, medicine, justice etc…

The Martyr Mambo

Now, where the Vampire Waltz is a two-way dance, the Martyr Mambo is more like a frozen drop pose - whereby one partner **offloads a 'pain' he or she is carrying onto the other's (usually) chest area**. The carrier then becomes the Energetic Martyr.

The pain is simply **unresolved energy – trapped emotion.** Remember, **emotion is energy in motion**. It is caused by anything from a traumatic situation, or an accident, verbal abuse, emotional abuse, living a lie, making a wrong decision, or simply being subscribed to a mass consciousness not aligned with you anymore. Basically, anything unresolved or unaddressed.

Note that this can easily happen by distance so please stay aware – and never assume it is only your problem, by calling this 'anxiety' for example. Why not keep track of who it happens in front of from now on? You will be surprised!

Projections are a common way to offload unresolved energy onto the martyr. For example, I remember one man saying to me "why is it all the women I attract…". I listened to his words and felt the energy start making its way over.

Thank goodness my BS meter intervened and said "no way, you are not carrying this trapped energy he has that he needs to resolve with his own inner female; you will not be that martyr for him!"

So, if you feel a heaviness when someone 'puts something' on you that is not yours, well, that something is a CHUNK OF UNRESOLVED ENERGY and here are four statements you can make to curb that ball - just command them in your mind, with emotional intent:

THE MARTYR'S ENERGY REMOVAL COMMAND

1. NO THANK YOU
2. IT IS NOT MINE
3. I SEND THE ENERGY BACK
4. IN ALL MY LOVE-POWER

It is also important to alert you to the fact that a Martyr Mambo can easily happen between you and collective ties too i.e. where the frustration of a mass-consciousness subscription is no longer serving that collective. Empaths or hyper-sensitives would carry this strongly. Unfortunately it is wrongly diagnosed as anxiety, but truth is, it is the martyr mambo en masse!

For example, I have felt the pains of the mass disregard of the female principle very deeply the last year or so, particularly how it has affected the Earth and her non-human inhabitants. I have truly felt her pain, and then wrath, her desire to push up and fight back at the mass disrespect. I wonder if you have felt this too? I have to say I worked diligently to remove the energy from my chest area for a few months, because it was binding me to The Matrix. But, first I had to remove my subscription to the 'victim status' of the female principle first! My tie to this is what allowed my energetic martyrdom to happen in the first place.

In Shopping Centres there are a lot of people needing to dance in a Martyr Mambo because of subscriptions to money, debt or lack. They actually really need a martyr! So if you are not aware, and you have a subscription to one of these mass belief systems yourself, you could easily find yourself carrying that nervous, anxious energy for others so: stay aware and trust your BS meter!

The thing is, if we are to help anyone at all, we must start with unbinding ourselves first – from individual cords and the collective's too – by checking in with our belief systems and shifting them emergently as we grow (until you no longer need any belief system whatsoever!).

The Signature of the Martyr

Some examples of signs of this form of martyrdom include:

- You feel a heaviness on your chest making it difficult to breathe – this can be called **'anxiety'** or a 'panic attack' – but it really means that you are very sensitive to people's feelings, sensitive to the live 'wires' of The Matrix. Every time you feel it your mind goes to that same person you are carrying it for (it could also be a nervousness in your tummy);

or, to the mass consciousness 'mindset' you are carrying it for.

- Your mind is stuck in replay mode – and it replays the situation over and over – this could go on for years (until the energy of it is processed)
- As with the vampire victim, any scenario where you leave feeling:
  - **Unheard**
  - **Undervalued**
  - **Invalidated**
  - **Disregarded**
  - **Disrespected**
  - **Unjustly treated**

How Dire is the Situation?!

The good news is that neither the Vampire Waltz nor the Martyr Mambo are PERMANENT (as highlighted in SACRED KEY 3). There is a way to sever these cords. But a note of warning – **as the wisdom of life dictates, they are there for a reason and**

can only be cut when it is optimal time –
which is when you as the master have gained
whatever knowledge you needed to – by
having that cord in place; and only then can it be
severed.

It's the Energy, It's so Powerful

"You torch me up
Like electricity
Jumpstart my heart
With your love "

Lyrics from 'Powerful', by Major Lazor

IT ALL STARTS WITH ENERGY.

Whatever will come into existence begins at the essence level – which is, the level from which energy exists.

This also holds for **dis-ease** – it **begins energetically**. So if your awareness is attuned to its most subtlest of abilities which is the energetic level, it will be able to pick up and deal with any DIS-CORD (get it?!) before it need manifest in the physical.

Animals do this well. If you have a pet dog, watch him. When he's been hurt or perturbed in any way, he'll do something akin to a sneeze. But it is not a sneeze. This is his way of removing the energy of his discord, immediately – in the moment, because otherwise it will remain trapped in his Vehicle of Consciousness; rather than what humans do – which is quite often hold it – simply because: we haven't developed that subtle awareness ability needed to work at the level of energy in the NOW-MOMENT – as it presents itself. And as the energy of discord builds, it WILL be felt – we call this the ELEPHANT IN THE ROOM... (Note: when animals do suffer dis-ease, it is because they have been sucked into The Matrix too – via an energetic cord which has formed with their owner(s)).

Building Your Energy Level of Awareness

For you to be able to work at preventing discord just like animals do, you need to deeply develop your subtle level of awareness. I want to assure you that this CAN be done easily and it starts by training your Energy Body (I'll talk more about this in the next chapter).

You can train your Energy Body just like you can train your physical body – why not, to get optimum wellbeing?

Working at energy level is DISEASE PREVENTION ON TURBO!

Please note that I do hold teaching circles on how to train your Energy Body, and of course you can learn through one of my personal coaching packages; but, regardless, **if you intend for this to happen – you will find YOUR way** regardless – with or without me.

So, how did I realize the cords were there?

The way I arrived at the revelations and wisdom that came along with them was by vigilantly following and most importantly ACKNOWLEDGING all of MY experiences as perfect for me – even when they HURT; even when they seemed to others like MISTAKES because they would lead me to getting hurt (and for anyone in the know of such phrases, I consciously used all the aches and pains spurred on by interactions with my Twin Flame to work on myself; I did not know it at the time, but this conscious choice was to help me birth this knowledge, move toward self-mastery at an alarming rate and expand my business into something I had never imagined!).

Truth is, averting 'mistakes' is just another blind mass subscription that held me back, so I tossed it. For I knew that my experiences were my essence's quest to simply arrive at its longed-for 'ease'.

Whether my experience was something I did or something that 'happened to me' – I observed all of it as if I was gathering data for an experiment of, I did not know what.

The thing is – our emotions are basically 'energy in motion'. Which means that if we take our awareness to them, we simply ALLOW the energy that has begun moving, to resolve its self.

As I observed the chaos of my mind, who it was thinking about, if it was obsessing – I also noticed the energy in motion at play in my body; and I listened to the words I uttered around each experience. I heard myself say things like: 'I'm trapped in this', 'I can't cut the cord', 'I feel bound to"… etc.

For example I began noticing the faulty exchange of energetic patterns at play from interactions with others whereby an uncomfortable, 'contractive' energy was 'set in motion' in my Vehicle. These interactions included for example, when a person verbally attacked me, advised me, judged me or emotionally hurt me in any way.

Planning Your Escape

"Life begins at the edge of your comfort zone"

Unknown

What symptoms accompany that push for your essence to be at ease, your essence seeking to escape The Matrix? Have you noticed?

Here's a not-so exhaustive list, as I merely desire to spark curiosity and suggest that if you are experiencing any of these, please do not discount that there may be something at play on an energetic level:

- Unease
- Bouts of 'ease', joy, bliss, happiness – that are not permanent
- Loneliness
- Disconnect
- Feeling trapped and like you need to escape from something but have no idea what
- Anxiety

- Depression

- Despair

- Clouded thinking, fogginess

- Emotional unrest

- Mental fatigue

- Mental overstimulation

- Arguing

- Feeling unhappy, despondent

- External blame

- Labelling yourself

- Tears for no reason

Whatever your symptoms are, they have your mind on alert. After all, you wonder, how could you possibly have any of these 'problems', since, by society's standards, you live quite a reasonably content existence? You have your family, your job, your home. You go on your holidays, have your fun. "What more do you want?' You ask your restless nudger!

Symptoms, a God Send

Before I go on, I would like to reframe the notion of mainstream's take on symptoms. This will be a MIND-OPENER for you, because so far, consensus mindset views symptoms as WRONG. But, I want to say to you: if what you were experiencing was wrong, you wouldn't be experiencing it; so the sheer fact that this is YOUR experience, means it is RIGHT for YOU.

So:

WHATEVER SYMPTOMS ARISE FOR YOU – MUST HAVE THEIR WISDOM

And that wisdom is something seeking to make itself known to your everyday self in order to get you back to ease. This is the way I approach my sessions as an awareness coach, and it provides such liberation to my clients. Because it is, ESSENTIALLY (which means at essence level!), true.

Your Vehicle of Consciousness (VOC)

Now remember from the introduction, you as CONSCIOUSNESSNESS seeking to fulfill itself, have four bodies in which to do this on THIS planet. From the most outer to the most inner, they are:

1. The Energy Body
2. The Mental Body (the 'mind')
3. The Emotional Body
4. The Physical Body

These four bodies make up your ONE VEHICLE OF CONSCIOUSNESS (VOC). When they are aligned and working optimally you ARE FULLY CONNECTED. Connected to your SELF, others, the planet and the universe.

The Energy Body provides you the energy you need to fuel your existence – it is at the root of your being.

Unfortunately, our Energy Bodies, since they have not been used properly for so long, actually need REHABILITATION. Just like when a person who has not walked for a long time needs to rehabilitate their Physical Body to walk again, so too must we rehabilitate the Energy Body to begin harnessing, flowing and using energy properly again.

A healthy Energy Body has energy flowing well through your central channel, meeting at your heart and from there flowing outwards as in figure 1.

Figure 1 - A healthy Energy Body and Central Channel down it's centre

Your central channel is an invisible tube that runs down the centre of your body from your crown down through to your perineum. Currently, it is not allowing energy to flow seamlessly into your heart, simply because your energy leaks out from your solar plexus – such that the energy is wasted - before it reaches the heart.

You can build an awareness with your Energy Body just like you have built one with your Physical Body. It communicates to you quite largely via EMOTIONS – which simply are: ENERGY IN MOTION. As I said earlier, any un-ease – that would eventually lead to dis-ease of your other bodies, starts nudging at you energetically first, initially very subtly. In other words, you sense it.

The Energy Body creates a **field** around you as previously mentioned.

You can work on building, strengthening and 'qualifying' (I will explain this concept later on) this field around you too. The more you do, the more you are extricating yourself from The Matrix.

Chances are, you probably have already started the extraction, but without realizing it. However, now, with the information in this book – the process becomes **CONSCIOUS**. And, as I said earlier, when something is brought to light by being brought to CONSCIOUS awareness – then energy, like a bullet, can be shot out of the gun of your awareness – able to strike at the now CLEAR target ahead.

Indeed targets are hit without your conscious awareness, but that is like shooting a gun without aiming – you send out bullets that sometimes hit the target, BUT, you definitely have a much higher chance of hitting that target when you **aim**.

The thing is:

ENERGY FOLLOWS AWARENESS

So, because, we are walking energy tanks, we are really like this big <u>BANK OF ENERGY</u>.

Anytime ANYONE has our ATTENTION they are getting our ENERGY.

Meaning, I want you from now on, to consciously choose who you want to GIFT your precious energy deposit via attention to that: person, TV show, news clip, magazine, photo-shopped Facebook selfie (haha) etc…

Because, the more often you put your attention to something or someone non-consciously, the greater the chance you have of BINDING YOURSELF to them, and so the more you get pulled into the heavy pollution of the faulty Matrix system.

Importantly, the energetic cords strengthen over time – which is why couples and family members stay stuck in their entangled relationships – because energetically, there is a cord that BINDS THEM, and it gets so difficult to get out.

Aaahhh those deep 'emotional ties' have a lot to answer for!

Power Games

"Power is the ultimate aphrodisiac."

Henry Kissinger

If you really look deeply, you will see that **life is one big game of energy exchange**.

Take money for example – all it is - is a physical representation of the ENERGY we EXCHANGE between each other.

If you see money simply as a form of energy exchange – which is seeing what it is from energy's standpoint - it takes the pressure off all that we've attached to it.

It relieves you of all the mental disarray that clings to the notion of it, so that you can then receive it and give it, in accordance with your true essence.

Because, if it is a form of energy exchange, then if the EXCHANGE IS NOT IN HARMONY as per the

LAW OF ENERGY ie if what you put in is not what you get out - it is FAULTY and will hightail your essence into restlessness to be sure.

Now, when you think about it – for many, the current relationship with money is faulty. We either work our butts off short-changing ourselves of our deepest need for work-life balance; or we over-spend on things we don't need, falling into the traps of marketers and advertisers; or we don't have enough, and just scrape along to survive...

Oh and let's not forget how we have banks, retirement funds, credit cards, and superfunds – syphoning hidden fees and costs like there's no tomorrow.

All this REFLECTS that this is how we relate to EACH OTHER – we either syphon each other's energy stores OR leak our energy to the 'syphoners' (remember the Vampire Waltz?) - un-consciously.

So of course the physical representation of the way we exchange our energy (the money system) is going to be faulty too – for this is what life is: an outer reflection of your inner self …

Which brings me to the next Sacred Key. It is the way out of the mess that is life as we know it. And it is something we can each do on an individual level.

SACRED KEY 5

 THE GAME CHANGER: You have the power to change the current human trajectory – toward global love, peace and abundance – by VOWING clean, conscious energy exchange between yourself, others and your belief subscriptions.

We can together form a race of human beings who know that their energy stores need not come from each other, but from the freely available abundant energy supply of the Universe.

Human beings so in tune with their BS meter, that they will not leak their power ever again by subscribing to any limiting mass consciousness.

In this way, we will be truly connected to Source – through our own cordless Matrix – rather than sourcing our energy supply from each other.

I wonder if this also explains why we have such pain of separation from SOURCE... Maybe it is our inner wisdom saying we have plugged into the wrong ENERGY SOURCE for so long – that of each other; rather than using Universal Free Energy as Source!

We can each aim to emerge from this faulty Matrix by absolving ourselves of those energetic ties that bind us both individually and collectively.

This IS the way, it is up to each of us – the government cannot make any laws or any changes to maintain a sustainable peaceful planet for the children of tomorrow. It is up to each one of us individually to take the stand, and WILL OURSELVES OUT.

We can do this – it is not difficult – all it needs is our awareness, our intent and our commitment to our own self-mastery. That is it!

If I could dream with you right now, I would ask you to consider – if we were obtaining our energy abundantly and freely – without it being syphoned without our awareness, and if our outer world reflects our inner, THEN, how then, would our money system look then?!!

Can you imagine? WE WOULD ALL BE BASKING IN ABUNDANCE, that is how it would look – there IS no other way!

Control Dramas are Power Games

Now, we NEED energy to EXIST– we USE it to manifest, to create, to experience. So the notion of energy indeed is highly important because – it is a non-negotiable for survival.

Why, look at how our outer worlds' manifestation of this NEED for energy has manifested – there is a huge dependency on containable energy such as electricity and fuel – for storing it, selling it, needing it and owning it.

Bringing this back to our inner need for energy and energy storage, this is why we have been getting energy from each other for years – because we need it to survive!

For those of you that have read The Celestine Prophecy by James Redfield, this knowledge is nothing new. James mentions how since **humanity has forgotten that energy is FREELY AVAILABLE, we've needed to get it from**

somewhere, and so we began to get it from each other.

James says that the way we all get it from each other all starts from within the role you play in your birth family. He calls this role a 'control drama' and says: we develop our 'control drama' during our childhood, depending on the roles of others within the family. Then we take it into our adulthood and replay the drama again and again and again with our family, friends, children, lovers and colleagues; until one day when we finally realize what we've been doing on repeat for so long!

For example, if our mother's role is the 'incessant control freak' – then that is how she gets energy – so you very well may have become the 'incessant people pleaser' because that is how you got attention.

Other control drama archetypes he mentions include: the 'interrogator', the 'victim', the 'detached', the 'people pleaser' or the 'intimidator'. There might be others, but that's another discussion – for now I want

to concentrate on – well, so we have these control
dramas – but how do we exactly obtain the energy?

Building on James' wisdom then I bring this to your
awareness: these control dramas really are just power
games; and we play them because they provide us
with attention. And as I mentioned earlier:

ATTENTION is ENERGY!

Overt 'attention seekers' get energy - that's why
some people find them annoying after a while –
because, they've plugged into your circuit if you've
allowed it, and they're powering up from your
energy bank, just because they got your attention.

Thing is, we may not be overt attention seekers – but
we've gotten attention anyway, through the role
we've played in our lifelong control drama.

Every time someone has your ATTENTION - whether
they are in front of you or not – there is an energy
exchange, because attention IS how we get energy.

So now you know why pouting breast showcasing bum pushing selfies are so viral – we all thrive on the energy we get from the attention!

Oh and celebrities, when we say any publicity is good publicity – it's true! Why? Because having the attention of the masses means more energy their way, which means more money their way, since money is the physical representation of energy exchange!

Now before you go all crazy pouting away on me or creating bad publicity for yourselves, I want you to take note: getting energy through attention this way is NOT OPTIMAL because it keeps you bound to The Matrix either way, even if you're benefitting for a short while. Why, look at the current disfigurement we see in so many celebrities' faces; where their race to 'save face' is a depiction of this... Not to mention, the demise of so many of them: Michael Jackson, Marilyn Munroe, and Elvis Presley to name a few.

Now don't worry, there is an optimal way – I found mine; and instead of me reducing it into a packageable format in order to capitalize on it - which will only detract you from your mastery - I prefer to merely offer you a SCAFFOLD and TOOL-KIT along with TEACHING & GUIDANCE - so that you find yours. This IS the only path to self-mastery... Finding YOUR way..

Remember, this faulty way of energy exchange is not only on an individual or family level. It has happened on a collective level too for thousands of years – hooking the masses' energy through royalty, rulers, government and in the last century through offline - and now online – media and marketing, sucking the masses into the web through energetically feeding celebrities and movie stars abundantly too!

Building Your Own Matrix

"You take the blue pill, the story ends, you wake up in your bed and believe whatever you want to believe. You take the red pill, you stay in Wonderland, and I show you how deep the rabbit hole goes."

The Matrix: The Shooting Script

Emerging out of The Matrix is akin to taking the red pill depicted in The Matrix movie. It is a new, unchartered space and as such, can be definitely unsettling.

Why even as I was waking this morning, I found myself wondering where my passion had gone – and then I realized: my passion used to be 'fuelled' by anger – I was doing the Vampire Waltz with two of the people I love the most in this world. Which meant, their love for me was such that I was syphoning energy from them for this book, for my work, for my life!

So, since I was no longer waltzing with them after consciously removing myself from The Matrix (and the ties to them), this new way of being, of getting energy, felt so foreign, I felt so lost!

Then that little bubble of excitement arose again – for this book, for life, for my work, for my mission; and I thought – oh yes, this IS perfect. Now that I'm not syphoning their energy unawares, I can go on fully committed to my mission in a more healthy, less gruesome way.

With more gentleness and balance. I know I can have it all. I know I can do what I love and enjoy my family. I know I can be that entrepreneur as well as that woman who loves and enjoys her home life too, and who doesn't have to move to the mountains to live in serenity and abundant joy. And so I will weave this truth. I will weave this reality. From inside my OWN matrix!

The way I now RELATE to the world – to time, to people, to life – it's different; and I'm just paving my way. But once I do – I will fill you in on what to expect – because the new framework that comes with your OWN MATRIX is mind-blowing. I know it will take some 'time' to get used to it all. But I'm going to keep spinning my web, regardless.

So there you go – who would have thought that a mathematician like me could even have a go at weaving her own magic with words, when numbers seemed so natural when she entered this plane... I'm glad I unsubscribed from that mindset – that polarizes humanity into abilities. You're 'Sciencey' – you go to the left, you're 'Artsy '– you go to the right. This is a hugely limiting mindset – ignore it, and emerge freely as you!

I must warn you though, initially The Matrix will try and pull you back in. Those same people you may have done the Vampire Waltz with or the Martyr Mambo – they will try harder than ever to reconnect that cord. Imagine how lost they would inherently feel now that it's gone.

This is apparent, you will see it play out in your relationships. But, it is nothing short of a miracle how quickly they will change too. Some may seamlessly disappear out of your life altogether – whatever is optimal for both parties really – but it all happens organically, without being forced or controlled.

What is important to remember as you enter your Cordless Rabbit Hole is that any last painful tugs from those most closely tied to you, are just providing you opportunities to strengthen your calibration to your new; to power yourself up in your own mastery.

The beautiful control dramas will still be playing out their own little script – and if you find yourself caught in them – that is perfect – because it shows you how easy it is to get sucked back into The Matrix if you are <u>caught unawares</u> – replaying the character role that has been on autopilot much of your whole life – whose lines you learnt so well, you just rattled them off again and again and again. Like a parrot.

Calibration Process

I cannot stress this enough, I know I just mentioned it, but please know that there is a process of **'calibrating'** to your new normal, and it can be quite challenging. You will find yourself caught unawares sometimes in either syphoning energy or supplying others energy; meaning you will swing between being sucked back into The Matrix to then being spat back out again; recalibrating to your new normal as you go.

This is not so much self-sabotage or an 'upper limit problem' as Gay Hendricks calls the discomfort met along the way into your Zone of Genius. It is simply a calibration to your NEW NORMAL, which, may I say, has a new form of ENERGY to it too as you will see – in fact any moments now that you feel expansive and absolutely joyous - that is this NEW ENERGY and it has already begun weaving its way into your life, because, as I have previously stated, you have already begun emerging from The Matrix even before reading this.

Signs of calibration to a new normal include getting a 'cold', or a cold sore, or having a 'down' day (or few). And, be warned, pent up tears will expel themselves from the bowels of your past as part of your catharsis; embrace them, nurture yourself, and understand that this is part of your journey.

Eventually, your need to cry from pain will be no more!!! You will no longer be carrying 'it' – the energy of **unresolved emotions** such as grief or trauma or whatever has remained stuck in your field for so long. While your Energy Body was weaker, there was no way it could process both the energy of unresolved emotions, and, extricate you from The Matrix too. Indeed, this changes as your Energy Body strengthens over time.

Know too that this calibration is because your Vehicle of Consciousness is preparing itself to hold more light – to increase its **light quotient**.

To be honest, that is technically the real reason for the calibration process and why all **the discordants to your new pending world have to be shed**.

During the calibration know that you will swing between extremes. Between extremes of: mental/emotional clarity then chaos; expansion and joy then despair and torment; absolute acceptance and trust then doubt and fear of lack.

Basically you will swing between moments of extreme expansion to moments of extreme contraction. This is all part of the calibration process. I'm shown it to be a swinging pendulum. So, you can rest assured - you will eventually come to harmonization in the middle, once your 'extremes' have been experienced.

Importantly, you will also have some sort of 'distraction' – perhaps a lover or pressing work issue for example - that can easily drag you away from the expansion process, and suck you back into The Matrix.

Please note also that you will experience greater sensitivity to energies so I ask you to pledge to yourself that you will not place yourself anywhere where it is energetically uncomfortable – especially energetically toxic. I like to say: we would not go about eating rat poison to poison our Physical Bodies, so why go about poisoning our Energy Bodies?

Growing out of the habitual Vampire Waltz and Martyr Mambo dances will take some time. You will watch the habit go into its little autopilot, then you will smile it away as you realize – you no longer want to partake in that power game anymore, because you are silently spinning your own cordless web.

What You Can Expect To Experience Once in Your Own Matrix

Once you have cut all ties, retrieved all power, patched up any leakages in your energy field, and prepared your Energy Body enough to be self-propelling (again I will be teaching and writing about this in my Blog and YouTube Channel), you will then begin to feel what it is like to be in your own Matrix.

There is more Energy Work to be had initially during the calibration process, but once you have your Energy Body going on its own, you are set!

You will experience a different way of being in yourself. Initially in small doses. The process is titrated – so the experiences will increase as you go on.

You will definitely feel **UNBOUND** – free – and begin to grasp just exactly how it feels to BE a master of your own universe. You will literally feel nothing attached to your field. It feels so light. It is actually breathtaking to be honest.

People will comment how free they feel around you too!

You will also experience the most beautiful powerful uplifting **energies** flowing into you, through you and extending out into your energy field and beyond.

An amazing sensation of **SPACIOUSNESS** will start to accompany you. It feels like you do not have a body, but that you are just part of everything – the whole room, whole city, whole world. It's difficult to explain but darn it feels good.

Surprisingly, you will begin to automatically start breathing through your **pineal gland** too – which sits behind the bridge of your nose - something Gregg Bradden mentions in 'The Ancient Secret of the Flower of Life'; but you actually feel it happening automatically which seems bizarre at first.

You will notice that people feel energized, healed and lighter after spending even ten minutes with you. This is the potential of all of us: to beam perpetually from within our own Cordless Matrix, for ourselves first, and in doing so, the overflow of our fullness in SELF, gifts the world around us…

You will experience yourself more and more as a Universal Citizen. You will connect with any other aspects of you across the Universe. You will understand your purpose more clearly, and may even experience your existence as a combined mission/holiday on this planet – like all your other existences.

You will find yourself not having to consciously do **energy work** as much, because it will be **happening for you automatically.** Just like breathing when you first got here must have felt unusual, now you don't even have to think about it, that's how a healthy Energy Body works too – effortlessly, seamlessly and organically.

All in all, you are calibrating to a new normal that is MAGICAL. The potential of which is limitless, for it means you are operating from outside the old Matrix.

It means you are a wireless little universe, all unto yourself, fuelled by nothing other than the abundantly available free energy that abounds in the universe.

Now you are even more advanced than those mobile phones, because unlike you, they still need an old-fashioned way of 'recharging'.

You just run off of 'thin air'...

THE HOW

It's time for you to Get Started! To emerge from The Matrix and begin to build your own!

Here is a handy list you can adopt to help you take the reins and get out:

1. Make and feel the **intention** to get out of it
2. Celebrate every experience as **right** for you
3. Follow your soul-forces – they are the tools through which you need to navigate your existence. They are:

DESIRE
CURIOSITY
PASSION

4. Observe linear thinking – it can be reductive ie it reduces your experience; you are a multi-dimensional being – you experience truth on several levels, all levels are right in their own 'light'

5. Practice breathing through your pineal gland consciously

6. **FOLLOW NATURE**. This is YOU. **YOU ARE NATURE** TOO – so **FOLLOW YOU**! How? Using your awareness. Remember, ENERGY FOLLOWS AWARENESS. So simply take your awareness and gently follow you, just like you would when observing 'nature'. You have a NATURAL STATE OF EASE – just like animals do; when this has been upset, follow your experience – wherever your mind goes, whatever you feel, whatever people say and or do whatever you hear etc – your SELF has created the whole experience in order to get your nature back to ease..

7. Keep your **BS METER turned on high**. When it gets stirred it will signal to you via uncomfortable energy in motion (=EMOTION) after hearing something for eg in the news, on radio, from a friend – pay attention to it. IF YOUR BS METER IS STIRRED, **LISTEN TO IT** – IT HAS YOUR BACK. It is telling you that you

may be being asked to dance the Vampire Waltz or Martyr Mambo without realizing it...

8. **Observe any Vampire Waltzes or Martyr Mambos** you might be dancing in unwittingly. Work yourself out of that dance using the solutions I gave you. Here's a recap of them:

ENDING THE VAMPIRE WALTZ

1. VISUALISE WITH FELT-INTENT DISSOLVING THE CORD TO THAT PERSON THAT CONNECTS TO YOUR SOLAR PLEXUS

2. VISUALISE WITH FELT-INTENT 'SEALING' THE 'HOLE' IN YOUR FIELD THAT CORD CREATED

THE MARTYR'S ENERGY REMOVAL COMMAND

1. "NO THANK YOU"
2. "IT IS NOT MINE"
3. "I SEND THE ENERGY BACK"
4. "IN ALL MY LOVE-POWER"

9. **Visualize a Violet Flame** (this is known as invoking St Germaine's violet flame) burning through any energetic debris in your four bodies, and especially your energy field. Do this daily to prevent any suctioning back into the faulty Matrix. The more pure you and your field, the less chance of it sucking you back in.

10. **Prepare for your ReSET: reprogram yourself** using the following felt-affirmations if you need to:

"I LOVE YOU"
"I RECEIVE IN GRATITUDE"
"I AM IN MY OWN MATRIX"
"I HEAL MY CENTRAL CHANNEL"
"NOTHING & NO-ONE BINDS ME"
"THIS IS MY FINAL RESET"

11. Feel and intend for **embodied interconnectivity** with all that is

12. Intend to **harmonize your own inner male and female**

13. Most importantly:

    Visualize yourself in your own healthy

clear Matrix; with your heart as your power tool:

 YOUR HEART AS YOUR POWER TOOL: Your heart is designed to be the generator and transmitter of energy.

As the energy enters up from the earth and down from the heavens into your heart, you must train your heart to transmit and generate the energy consciously. This '**qualifies**' your energy stock, making your vibe irresistible to you and others indeed!

The good news is, once you have your Energy Body rehabilitated and working healthily again, your heart will be able to do this naturally. However, initially, you must consciously get your heart transmitting and generating the energy for you (again I will post exercises on how to do this on my YouTube channel).

Remember, a healthy Energy Body has energy flowing well through your central channel, meeting at your heart and from there flowing outwards as in the figure 1 below.

Figure 1 - A healthy Energy Body and Central Channel down it's centre

Furthermore, you must work on **expanding** your heart, for your heart also acts as the **ENERGY PURIFIER**. What this means is – because your hearts generate and transmit energy – where you heart sits – toward your self AND towards life, determines the QUALITY of your energy. Think about it – your energy is your FUEL. So if you are running on low grade fuel, you are simply not running at MAXIMUM CAPACITY. You are not soaring to your truest potential!

Make your fuel premium by setting the intent to **expand your heart**. The stages for this include:

- removing energy blockages around it
- removing or reprogramming mindsets that limit it's capacity to love
- consciously working on EXPANDING it's ability to love.

There is no end-point to your heart's capacity to love by the way. In fact, it has the capacity for an infinite amount of love expansion!

Actually, the energy is meant to meet at your heart, where your heart then both generates more energy AND transmits it out into your Matrix.

The way I'm shown this looks like, is a series of concentric (i.e having the same centre) infinity symbols – whose centre is your heart, as shown in Figure 2 (excuse the amateur drawing!).

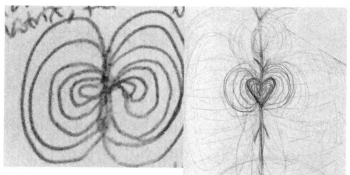

Figure 2 – Healthy energy flow around our heart looks like concentric infinity symbols, making us human angels!

So a healthy Energy Body with a clear central channel and a powerful generating-transmitting heart looks like Figure 1.

Which brings me to my final and most liberating SACRED KEY. But before I introduce it, I want you to look closely behind the heart area in Figure 1; and then again at Figure 2...

Do you notice anything? Have you realized anything? Does the healthy energy field that crosses at the heart look like it creates – from a 2D perspective – what could be taken as WINGS?!

THE ULTIMATE KEY TO ASCENSION:
When you are in your **own healthy self-propelling cordless Matrix with a** healthy Energy Body, powerful heart and unobstructed central channel, you begin your Ascension Journey. You literally become A **HUMAN ANGEL.**

To Universal Citizens that can <u>see</u> energy, if they were to look at us front on, our perfectly formed energy field – the way it propels out from your heart, would have us looking like we have wings, just like angels, but human angels!

So there you have it, you have just been given the keys to ascension! In your own cordless Matrix, you will start to **ascend – simply because, like a helium balloon, nothing is binding you energetically anymore. This is what ascension means!**

Ascended Masters are simply beings like you and I who figured out how to break free of any Matrix in order to be self-propelling conscious beings who obtain their energy supplies directly from Source.

Can you believe it?! It IS possible for us to EMBODY the same state such as all those 'Master' beings we humans have revered for so long; that we placed far outside of our reach: the Ascended Masters. Jesus, Buddha, St Germain...

What's more: **as Ascended Masters on planet Earth, what we simply end up realizing, is that we truly are: Human Angels!**

Afterword

Getting to the level of being in your own matrix – and mastering your own energy supply takes quite a journey. It takes a lot of un-learning, un-programming, unsubscribing – to many of the beliefs/mindsets that held you captive in The Matrix for so long.

Because once you've unsubscribed from these belief systems, you are, as a master of your own existence, then, able to set up a NEW FRAMEWORK for relating – one that then creates the SCAFFOLD for your magical existence to blossom.

I want you to remember – any framework, scaffold, systematized ANYTHING – should NEVER BE PERMANENT – should only provide a platform from which to emerge onto your next level of expansion and growth.

For if it were to remain, you would remain there – at that level. And expansion, emergence – is infinite. The possibilities are endless.

So create the scaffolds for aspects of your new cordfree existence for areas such as work, relationships, money, etc; then, as the magic takes over – bless each scaffold – kiss it goodbye, and let yourself fly in the overflow of you, as you emerge, freely, wholly, unbound and limitless.

Abundance with abandon your due...

Postscript

You Hold In Your Hands Something Special

I hope you can see that this is more than just a book. This knowledge, I have been told, has remained hidden for thousands of years, waiting for the right time to surface. It is for this reason that it is sacred. And as such, you my dear reader must treasure it accordingly.

What you hold is a GOLDEN KEY for humanity.
A key that unlocks eons of entrapment.
A Bridge born to form a direct link from Heaven to You.

So I ask you this:
PLEASE PROTECT THIS SACRED KNOWLEDGE, MY GOLDEN CHILD.

Please share it only with those your BS meter says too! For, were it to get into the wrong hands – this knowledge would surely be shut down – which would be a tragedy that could set humanity back in a myriad of ways.

The way humanity is going now, the way the faulty Matrix is shown to me – is truly NOT SUSTAINABLE. So I beg you please – guard this knowledge with all your heart. For each of us, by having it, will slowly awaken others – but only when they are ready can they digest this.

I am told by my non-physical Ascension Mission Team, that with this knowledge, together we will create a grass-roots movement.
We will silently build a peace corps.
With training we can do SILENTLY, in our everyday!
A tribe of emPOWERed people
Who CAN NOT be harmed.
With this knowledge they tell me, we change the current trajectory of the human race.
This IS OUR GAME CHANGER.

WELCOME TO YOUR POWER

About Me

Hi there ☺

OK, I'm going to be straight up: I used to be a mathematician – programming mathematical & statistical models for real world problems.

Now I use that ability on individuals and the collective: I dive into the depths of a story's complexity, park the variables and solve for the constant: the distilled wisdom.

I do it on philosophy too. Always seeking to solve, resolve, understand, reduce, and then expand.

I'm also an artist. Poetry, well, writing - is my art.

We all have that artist deep inside… waiting to be

expressed and experienced.

The moment I embraced the mathematician in me

with the artist AND the sagacious lover of humanity,

I found real expression and expansion, the likes of

which I never knew possible.

The lens I bring is highly out of field, to the point

where people find themselves lost in a string of 'Aha'

moments through my discussions, teachings, words

and dialogue.

I am the Resident Re-framer!

Because I re-frame things, take them out of Polarity

Consciousness, back into Unity Consciousness,

I must say it took quite a few soul-piercing

experiences to sculpt my lens to be as wide as it is

now.

Before the tsunami of grief smashed at the shores of

my mundane existence, I was quite content living

within narrower confines of my self.

Until the wisdom of life reared its darker head, there

was one loss after another: my childhood innocence,

a stillborn child, my sister at 34, and then my

marriage – the unfortunate casualty - swallowed along by the force of the debris …

Merging all my aspects has meant I have had to embrace MYSTERY.

Life has no meaning without it.

It has allowed me to bring voice to the UNSPOKENS in life - for once we bring them to light, we are set for collective healing, the likes of which we only ever dreamt about.

Oh and the mystery I have been able to bring my voice to!

Working in the abstract world of numbers for so long meant that my mind was open to the most unlikely of discoveries. Here's one big one:

Personal development is nothing without training your Energy Body!

For years I was working on my Energy Body, unsure as to why. It was just something that came naturally.

Until people started commenting – saying "What's your secret? Is it a new man?" People I'd meet simply would not believe my age, some even asking me for ID for proof!

I realized this must be the energy work, and, of course bringing it to the planet is a big part of my mission.

So now I'm this '**mathematical gypsy**' that teaches about 'Energy Mastery' for 'Self Mastery'; who's created a formula for personal growth that leads right up to the ultimate of heights –

Embodied Empowerment.

And so, I'm truly thrilled you have joined me in my Empowering You rEvolution.

Welcome!

With Love,

– Katrina

June 2015

If you would like to hear more about my personal journey, I have decided to share it with you openly, in raw form (so grab some tissues!):

http://sacredmysteries.com.au/awakening-through-grief-my-story/.

How Can you Work with Me?

Please visit the 'Work with Me' section on my website:

http://sacredmysteries.com.au/work-with-me/

Or please **EMAIL ME** for more information!

Sacred Mysteries YouTube Channel

I also have a Sacred Mysteries Youtube Channel which you can find under **KatrinaTV** on my website! It has all my latest tranmissions, wisdom and energy updates!

Contact Details

Email: info@sacredmysteries.com.au

Skype: KatrinaLoukas

Web: http://sacredmysteries.com.au

About Self Mastery and Energy Mastery

One aspect of my mission is to teach people how to master their SELVES. This simply means helping those committed to PERSONAL GROWTH & TRANSFORMATION, who seek OPTIMAL, EXCEPTIONAL, PERMANENT results, on ALL levels of their existence.

Energy Mastery is an important aspect of self-mastery. In fact, **self-mastery STARTS with 'energy work'. We've got it ass-end up when we start with the physical or mental aspects first!**

Because working on the ESSENCE of existence, the energetic level, means that it then CASCADES into the mental, emotional then physical bodies, and then, into every aspect of your existence: love, money, work, family and your self. So essentially, you're fixing things at root level when you do energy work!

Energy Mastery Training

My Energy Mastery Training consists of 3 levels from the Introductory '100 Series' program right through to the Advanced '300 Series' program.

The training is **integrated** into my work with individual clients, speaking engagements or corporate consultations and seminars.

However, I have created easy, accessible, do-it-yourself **Workbook Bundles for Only $17** available on my **Online Store.** These bundles are a must-have with this book!

About Sacred Mysteries™

Sacred Mysteries is dedicated to delivering methods for ultimate personal growth, the type of empowerment that comes from your body, not only your head!

Our mission is to create authentic community - to help change the current trajectory of the human race, towards one full of magical citizens who bask in ever-lasting peace.

Our values we call our non-negotiables. Firstly, we are **trail-blazers** – we dare to blaze our own trail for the highest good of all, without compromise. We do this in **love-power**, with **integrity** and **compassion**. We remain **emergent** – we will not get stuck with being SET in our ways, but instead choose to grow with the currents of the time. Lastly, and importantly, all our decisions stem from a **unity** mindset, from a place of *no division*.

Contact Details

Email: info@sacredmysteries.com.au

Skype: KatrinaLoukas

Web: http://sacredmysteries.com.au

Bonus Gift!:

Here's a poem I wrote for every time you need that kick-ass affirming power shot to validate when you will not apologize for being YOU!

I WILL NOT APOLOGIZE: A WOMAN'S PLEDGE

I will not apologize:
For being a woman
For needing tenderness and love
Empathy and compassion;
For needing my inner space.

I will not apologize:
For needing to be heard
For needing companionship and understanding
Equanimity and equality;
For needing my inner space.

I will not apologize:

For my monthly menses

For feeling pain and exhaustion

For needing time to rest and recharge;

For needing my inner space.

I will not apologize:

For my looks

For my hair or features

For my shape or height;

For needing my inner space.

I will not apologize:

For my sense of mothering

For shouting words of encouragement

Along the soccer field

To my over smothering and nurturing;

For needing my inner space.

I will not apologize:

For FEELING!

For expressing what hasn't been said

For crying tears of frustration

At not having been heard or understood;

For needing my inner space.

ALL OF THIS I NOW KNOW:
Thanks to my inner space

THANKS TO MY INNER SPACE
I WILL NOT APOLOGIZE FOR SO MUCH MORE:

I will not apologize:
For needing to make love
Not just have sex
For needing passion and connection;

I will not apologize:
For being connected with my heart:
MY compass – who offers me fullness and joy;
Without whom life is EMPTY.

I will not apologize:
For loving the earth
For feeling her pain
At disregard and disrespect.
For now I know:
Her pain has ALWAYS been mine.

I will not apologize:
For steering my son toward his heart
Rather than telling him
To stop crying
And be a man!

I will not apologize:
For wanting to live love in my everyday
For needing a heightened sensual experience
Even when I eat my food.

I will not apologize:
For offering a suggestion
That may lack the harshness
Of mainstream's distorted notion of 'reality';
For I – a Goddess – WILL compassion
And I WILL NOT settle for anything less.

And I KNOW:
If I don't OWN MY POWER OF WRATH:
Where will the children of tomorrow dwell?
In a world devoid of feeling,
Devoid of love, of regard, of depth, of sensuality,

Of compassion, of empathy?

In a world called:

ZOMBIELAND

NO WAY.

NO.

I – an expression of the

Female principle

In physical form;

A living embodiment

Of the GODDESS OF CREATION:

STEP INTO THE POWER OF MY WRATH

And say :

NO MORE!

For, with my sisters –

We rise empowered.

Awake.

And we DEMAND TO BE HEARD

ACKNOWLEDGED,

And UNDERSTOOD.

For the children of tomorrow

Depend on it.

Katrina <3

PS: This poem is ALSO FOR MY BROTHERS who –
with UTMOST COURAGE – DO NOT APOLOGIZE
for their INNER GODDESS = their natural
experiences of COMPASSION, LOVE,
NURTURING and EMOTION OVERALL!

Why not share it with your friends? You can find the
link here:
http://sacredmysteries.com.au/i-will-not-
apologise-a-womans-pledge/
BECAUSE YOU ARE SACRED

Join the Empowering YOU rEvolution!

Like Us on Facebook: 👍 Sacred Mysteries Facebook Page

Join our private tribe on Facebook: THE POWER PACK (by request only): The Power Pack

Join our private membership club, The Hood, for authentic co-creation: http://SacredMysteries.com.au.

References

Bradden Greg, 1998. The Ancient Secret of the Flower of Life. Light Technology Publishing, Arizona.

Henricks Gay, 2009. The Big Leap. Harper Collins, New York, NY.

Kenyon Tom, 1996. The Hathor Material. ORB Communications, Orcas, WA.

Redfield James 2011. The Celestine Prophecy. Transworld Publishers, Australia.

St Germain Adamus 2012. Live Your Divinity. Weiser Books, San Fransisco, CA.

St Germain Adamus, 2007. Masters of the New Energy. Weiser Books, San Fransisco, CA.

Polona Aurea Dawn: https://www.youtube.com/user/ASCENSIONPIONEERS

Figure 1 Artist Amoraea: www.divine-blueprint.com

CPSIA information can be obtained
at www.ICGtesting.com
Printed in the USA
LVOW13s0254020517
532923LV00034B/1909/P